Meditation Magic

Yoga and Meditation for the 3rd Millenium

Copyright Janie May Still 2011

Contents

Authors Note..Page 4

Chapter 1 Meditations Real Effects On Health............Page 9

Chapter 2 The Body Electric...............................Page 15

Chapter 3 Preparation – Posture – Breathing.............Page 29

Chapter 4 Concentration – Mantras – Pineal Gland...Page 37

Chapter 5 Chakra Awareness................................Page 45

Chapter 6 Yoga and weight-loss............................Page 57

Chapter 7 Systematic Under-eating........................Page 65

Chapter 8 Your Second Brain...............................Page 79

Chapter 9 Trust Your Body..................................Page 85

Chapter 10 Science and Consciousness....................Page 91

About the Author...Page 95

The Energy of Love..Page 101

Bibliography..Page 105

" Meditation has been shown to be able to play a part in relieving a host of mind-made illnesses, from anxiety to heart disease. " Dr Malcolm Carruthers

Authors Note

At the time of writing (February 2011) there has been a lot of media coverage attesting to the powerful, life-changing affects that the practise of meditation can bring about. Having been a practitioner of both, yoga and meditation for over thirty years, I too would like to add my voice to the growing acceptance of the truth of such encouraging statements.

During this early stage of the 21st Century with all the turmoil and chaos worldwide that we are subject to, I feel it imperative that each one of us do what it takes to bring about a reversal in the way we think and act: through meditation we are able to do this.
Without a crucial change from within we cannot hope to alter the destructive, downward, spiralling course that we are presently on.
I realize that to change one's long-held beliefs and thoughts is one of the most difficult task's of all, but with thousands of people worldwide that have accomplished this amazing feat you must believe that it is possible for you too.
It is comforting to witness in just the last decade the transition of meditation from being thought of as "esoteric" and therefore not available to all, to becoming increasingly accepted by the mainstream and attractive to people from all walks of life.
The tremendous rise in stress levels, particularly in the west, has added to its appeal. As more and more of us experience for ourselves the mental and physical changes that meditation can induce, the more able we will be to help our loved ones and those around us to find inner peace and in turn create a far better world for our children to inherit.
However, although it is important that we work towards the reduction of stress, for the serious student, meditation is about so much more than a tool used for this purpose alone.

Sitting in stillness for prolonged periods will encourage an inner calmness that leads to a greater understanding of who you are, you reach beyond superficiality to a much deeper level, a place of wisdom and love.
No academic qualifications are necessary to reach this exalted space within, nor, indeed are of much help.
It is said to be the most difficult mission for man to accomplish and can only be found through sheer effort and earnest desire. Meditation is the bridge we must cross to achieve this.
For some of us, the odyssey within our-self will often prove to be uncomfortable. We have become so accustomed to the incessant din of contemporary living that sitting quietly in stillness for more than a few moments is quite a challenge.
Lot's of unwanted thoughts and feelings will surface and may even be painful.
These difficulties will pass as you progress, patiently confronting and then discarding outgrown attitudes and perceptions to reveal the essential, divine part of YOU.
So dear reader, fasten your belt and prepare for a voyage of a life-time (and beyond) toward a different level of consciousness in readiness for your evolutionary advancement.

****

" Focusing on the act of breathing clears the mind of all daily distractions and clears our energy enabling us to better connect with the spirit within"…….Author Unknown

"Never regard your study as a duty, but as the enviable opportunity to learn to know the liberating influence of beauty in the realm of the spirit for your own personal joy and to the profit of the community to which your later work begins"……………….Albert Einstein

Chapter One
Meditations Real Effects on Health

Some people use meditation for spiritual growth or to find inner peace. Others use it as a means for relaxation and stress reduction. Whatever category applies to you, meditation is when you deliberately attempt to free yourself from the continuous stream of thoughts flowing through your mind. Focus on liberating your mind of all its conscious thoughts and simply watch the movement of the breath entering the nostrils into the trachea and down into the lungs.
The never-ending stimulation of our daily lives, visually, mentally, physically and emotionally wreaks havoc on our health. Meditation provides a way to give your mind a rest and allows it to focus on one thing only, without a volley of external distractions, or on nothing at all.
Numerous scientific studies have confirmed the health benefits of meditation. In one study published in 2003 in 'Psychosomatic Medicine', researchers found that regular meditation can boost the immune system. Participants of the study showed signs of increased activity in the areas of the brain related to positive emotions.
Other research has shown meditation to be effective against a variety of disorders including: stress, tension, anxiety and panic, high blood pressure, chronic pain, headaches, respiratory problems such as emphysema and asthma, sleep disturbances, gastrointestinal

problems, fatigue, skin disorders, mild depression, premenstrual syndrome and irritable bowel syndrome. Regular practitioners of meditation say that they have increased mental abilities and renewed vitality and have much less need to visit their doctor then before they began to meditate.

Studies have even shown that meditation can reduce or reverse cardiovascular disease and improve the ability to cope with chronic illness.

Making the time for meditation can be a problem for some at first.

With so many other things and people to attend to it may even seem impossible. But don't be put off if that is the case for you, start with yoga. When the physical body is prepared through yoga asanas, the mind becomes more malleable, easier to quiet. Yoga is thought of as meditation in action and that is what it is when we are centered in our practice.

Meditation is an exercise like a scientific experiment – you do it and see what the results are. Find a teacher or someone that knows more than you for advice and guidance – and keep going. Then as you begin to feel the tangible change taking place, you'll understand.

"When the mind and body have been purified through meditation, through truth, through understanding and simplicity, then the perfect behold the self, pure and brilliant"………………..Mundaka Upanisad

With the advancements in brain imaging and other techniques scientists have discovered that mental training through meditation can change the inner workings of the brain and allow people to achieve different levels of awareness.

By working with Tibetan monks, scientists have been able to translate mental experiences into a scientific language of high frequency gamma waves and brain coordination and identify the left prefrontal cortex of the brain – an area just behind the left forehead – as a place where brain activity associated with meditation is particularly intense.

In one study, scientists hooked up eight of the Dalai Lama's most accomplished practitioners (with an estimated 10,000 to 50,000 hours of meditation training) and ten student volunteers (with one week of training) for electroencephalograph (EEG) testing and brain scanning. The subjects were fitted with a net of 256 electrical sensors and asked to meditate on unconditional compassion for short periods of time. The sensors picked up slight bursts of electrical activity – caused by thinking and other mental motion – as large groupings of neurons sent messages to each other. The results found that sensors picked up much greater activation of fast-moving, powerful gamma waves in the monks, compared to the students.

The movement of the waves through the brain were better organized and coordinated in the monks than in the students.

The highest levels of gamma waves were found in monks who spent the most years meditating; intense gamma waves have been associated with knitting together dissimilar brain circuits and are connected to higher mental activity and heightened awareness.

It was concluded that meditation not only alters the workings of the brain in the short-term, but quite possibly permanently.

Armed with this information, the wondrous effects to our health and the awakening of otherwise dormant parts of the brain, surely is motivation enough to inspire you to begin to learn to meditate.

"It cannot be attained by the weak,Nor by the half-hearted,
Nor by a mere show of detachment. But as ,strength, stability, and inner freedom to grow,So does self-awareness grow.
Mundaka Upanisad

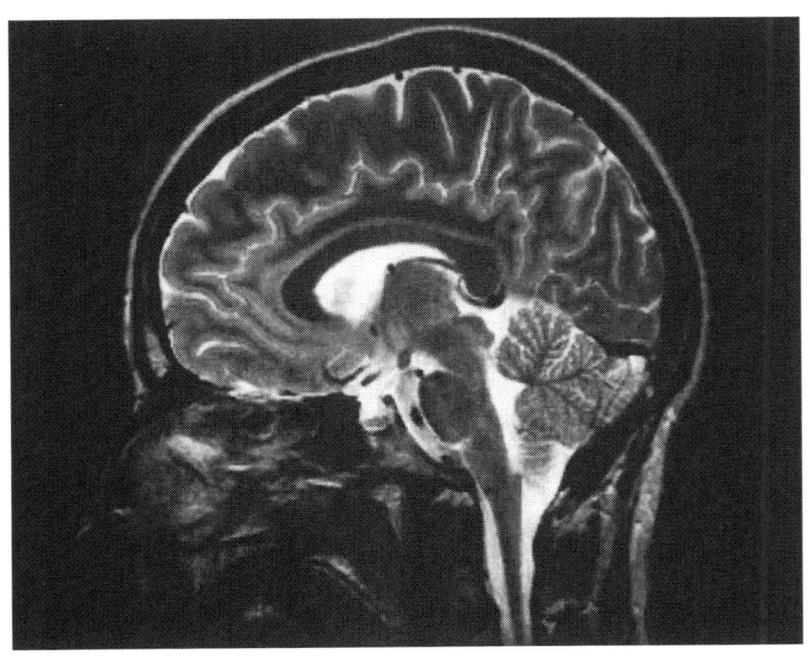

"Human beings can attain a worthy and harmonious life only if they are able to rid themselves, within the limits of nature, of the striving for the wish of material kinds. The goal is to raise the spiritual values of society."
Albert Einstein

Chapter two

The Body Electric

The new science of bioelectromagnetics has clearly established that we are fundamentally electromagnetic beings. In the 1960's, US scientist Robert Becker, a pioneer in EMF's and their effects on the human body stated that our bodies have their own very-low-level natural EMF's and that these fields are used by the body in many self-healing processes. Becker's discoveries were later reinforced by the work of German physicist Fritz-Albert Popp and the late French biologist Jacques Benveniste, who both independently showed that all the cells of the body communicate through subtle electromagnetic and quantum frequencies.

Their findings therefore make it plausible that we are being adversely affected by external EMF's. Before 1900, the earth's electromagnetic field was composed simply of the field made up primarily of visible light and random discharges of lightning compared to the field of today which has become a sea of energy that is almost totally man-made", explains Dr Robert O. Becker in his informative book, 'Cross Currents'.

I am convinced that the electromagnetic smog that has been created over the past 50 years is having a significant affect on all of us in lesser or greater degrees.

Increasing scientific evidence points to a close link

between the huge sudden rise in the amount of people suffering from neurological illnesses: Alzheimers, autism, anxiety disorders, parkinson's disease, muscular dystrophy, multiple sclerosis to name a few.

The electromagnetic pollution that is emitted from items in our home, work and outside environments i.e. power lines, mobile masts etc; means that we are all now exposed to electromagnetic fields (EMFs) in far greater amounts than nature intended.

Because EMFs are invisible and insensible doesn't mean that we can allow ourselves to be complacent about their possible effects.

You can't see them, hear or feel them, but we are bathed in them 24 hours a day.

Apart from the air itself, electromagnetic fields are the most pervasive things in our environment, and yet few of us give them a second thought.

Scientists in Russia have done more studies on EMFs than any other country and for decades have been reporting that electric fields cause high blood pressure, chronic stress effects, immune system dysfunction, changes in white and red blood cell counts, increased metabolism, chronic fatigue disorders and headaches. Other maladies that are thought to be caused by EMF's include loss of concentration and short term memory, depression, breathlessness, excessive thirst, numbness and a 'prickling' or weakness of the joints, leading to chronic, severe pain such as in fibromyalgia.

Dr Robert Becker sees a remarkable parallel between

those suffering from electro-sensitivity (ES) and the symptoms of multiple chemical sensitivity (MCS). Another increasingly prevalent environmental illness, caused by exposure to toxic chemicals such as pesticides. Both have the characteristics peculiar to immune-system disorders caused by a toxic overload (Dr Becker, Cross Currents).

Even more concerning, is the finding that mobile-mast radiation can affect DNA. Laboratory tests using human cells have shown that mobile-phone radiation is 'genotoxic'- able to interfere with cellular chromosomes and DNA.

Humanity has had millions of years of evolution but, in the space of just 50 years, we have rapidly become exposed to huge amounts of artificial electromagnetic radiation.

While it is true that we evolved in an EM environment – mostly radiation from the sun and the earth's magnetic field - these natural fields are very different from the EMFs produced by electric power . Could the assault of EMF's on the body affect our very cells by weakening the protective membrane.?

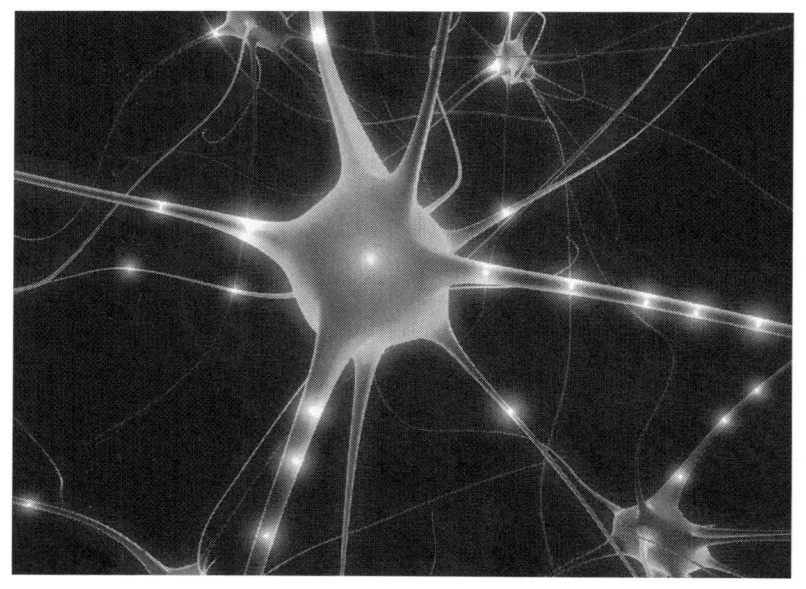

At the head of these new discoveries and insights comes the establishment of the facts that electricity is composed of discrete particles of equal size, or quanta, and that light is an electromagnetic wave motion.
Johannes Stark

The 21st Century has given us technology beyond our wildest dreams, however, this technology has also created some very unwelcome side-effects. None more so than the previously mentioned, suffusion of electro-magnetic-pollution in the environment.
Modern physics recognize that DNA emits it's own electromagnetic signals, and I believe that by strengthening our biological systems through focus and sincere intent we are able to offset the pernicious effects of artificial, electromagnetic currents and also the influx of extreme amounts of solar energy predicted for this period of existence.
Over time, meditation speeds up the body's vibration bringing it more in harmony with outside influences.
 Linda Goodman, an avatar of our time, wrote this insightful passage in 'Star Signs,' 1975:
"Your body was gloriously designed by your spirit, as your spirit's body was gloriously designed by your Creators, to be eternal. Your flesh body is a self-sustaining electromagnetic battery, forever capable of being recharged with energy, continually improved and transmuted into perfection through the process of cell-regeneration. And it all begins in your mind".
****

As stated, we are electromagnetic beings, our thoughts also are electromagnetic. Which begs the question; exactly to what extent is the manmade electromagnetic currents that permeate the atmosphere affecting not only our bodies, but our every thought too.? The answer to that will no doubt be forthcoming sooner than we might think, as there are presently various, scientific studies being carried out in many countries across the world by both pioneering individuals such as the aforementioned German physicist Fritz Albert Popp and US scientist Robert Becker, and prestigious establishments like The Karolinska Institute, Sweden, Oxford University, UK, The University of Washington, Seattle, and the University of Saarland, Germany, to name but a few.

****

There are now hundreds of people suffering from the overload of EMF's called 'electro-sensitives, who find this effusion of radiation so disabling that they cannot possibly live a normal life. Their symptoms range from headaches to chronic fatigue.

It's thought possible that as much as three percent of the population suffer from extreme adverse reactions to EMF's, called electrohypersensitivity (ES) and are often dismissed as being hypochondriacs.

But with the solid evidence of the harmful effects of EMF's gathering pace, will they continue to be dismissed so arrogantly. ?

"An investigation into the characteristics of the left and right sides of the human brain reveals certain anomalies. Facts about how our brains work coupled with such oddities such as handedness, sleepwalking and religious experiences are all clues to a 'second system' hidden within us that has a higher level of abilities than we realise. A new theory of how this may have arisen explains why accessing this second system is not straightforward. Over the course of our evolutionary history we have suffered a deleterious change in our consciousness that has affected not only how we act but also who we are. The consequences of this are far-reaching."

The preceding paragraph is an excerpt from "Left in the Dark" by Graham Gynn and Tony Wright. I include this profound passage as it pertains directly to the effects of meditation.

I believe that through the consistent practise of meditation we can connect to the "second system" they speak of, that higher level of ability and intelligence. It is our birth right, our duty that we do so in this life-time.

" The mind is everything; what you think, you become." Buddha

Plant the seed of meditation and reap the fruit of peace of mind.   Remez Sasson

That is by no means to reduce the discipline of meditation to just another chore to endure, not at all, for when we commit ourselves to learn to meditate we set in motion a series of events that will manifest and assist us with our determination to see it through.
Beside the more common reasons for learning to meditate: to reduce stress levels, to become more calm, to lower blood pressure etc; the latest, general consensus from the more enlightened of the scientific community is that the extraordinarily high levels of electromagnetic pollution caused by radio and TV signals, microwave transmissions, high power pylons and radiation that we are being subjected to in the 21st century is unprecedented and is causing serious damage to our bodies which then affect our defences against illness and disease .
So through systematic meditation practise we can physically protect the innermost part of the body from outside intrusions such as manufactured EMF's.
Until now, life on Earth was sustained by a natural electromagnetic environment which is being severely compromised.
The late Dr David James said: "If the amount of electromagnetism mist surrounding us were visible we would be unable to see a hand in front of our eyes"!.
I also believe that when we acquire the ability, through pure intention and persistence to draw our attention within ourselves, we become so empowered and in-tune with All-That-Is, Creator, God, (what ever name you are comfortable with) and it's that

communication that then strengthens the subtle bodies encircling us to such an extent as to stave off any ill-health that may otherwise befall us.

I, myself am living proof of this, I live just a few metres from a busy railway station, mobile masts and satellite dishes, all emitting harmful energetic frequency's that should, by all accounts be detrimental to my well-being. But compared to some of my friends that do not meditate and live in large houses in the countryside, away from these negative forces, I am extremely fit and healthy, whereas they are forever suffering from one illness or another.

****

We are living at a time in evolution that is prompting us to acknowledge that we are spiritual beings living in a human body and that our soul is infinite and will continue on it's personal so-journ until it reaches the blissful state of perfection.

When we pass over we will not be judged by our mistakes whilst on Earth but by how far we have evolved spiritually. Think about that for a moment.

Throughout our lives we are constantly told that after death we will be subject to harsh judgement pertaining to how good or bad we have been.

Upon discovering that it is solely our individual, spiritual development that matters, that the results of our dogged pursuit of a higher consciousness is what truly counts, is extraordinary. Meditation is the key that will lead us to this revered place where miracles are possible.

It's important to realise that no amount of reading and learning can teach us meditation, regardless of intellect or knowledge. All meditation teachers emphasise the importance of practise over theory, of first-hand knowledge over belief.

" Meditation is the basis of all inner work"…..Swami Durgananda

Although it is often said that sitting in stillness and silence can be one of the most difficult and daunting tasks for us to master, particularly in this frenetic age, it is my intention that after adhering to the following requirements, you will discover that that is the exception, not the rule .

Let me add that by letting go of any preconceived ideas that you may have, the easier these instructions will be to follow.

They have been written for those of you that are ready to connect to something greater than the present reality, to the Universal Mind that contains ALL.

"An ounce of practise is worth ten tons of theory"
Swami Vishnu Dev

Chapter Three

Preparation-Posture-Breathing

To prepare for meditation you must first make the TIME to practise . With the constant demands on our time we must learn to discriminate between what is necessary in our lives and what is not. Establishing a routine will be of great help. Develop the right habits from the beginning, ie; posture, breathing and the right frame of mind.
When you have been a practitioner for awhile, you will be able to meditate any time, anywhere.
By devoting some time to meditate – even just for a few minutes, you will feel a difference in your energy levels and more able to cope with life's challenges.
It is often advised to choose to meditate at dawn or dusk, these being the most auspicious times of day, when we are more receptive to the subtle, meditative energies.
If this is your first attempt at meditation it is wise to increase the time spent slowly.
Creating your very own space to meditate can really add to your practise, the place becomes infused with your unique energy and vibration.
Choose a quiet room or corner where you are warm and comfortable and make it personal by placing anything that you find inspiring: candles, pictures, incense, music or flowers, retain this space for your meditation practise only.

The more you practise there the more the positive energies will accumulate, allowing you to relax automatically as soon as you enter.
You must grant yourself permission to meditate and make it a priority, meditation is a discipline.
During the early stages of your practise the results may be felt mainly on a physical level, feelings of well-being and deep relaxation, but as you progress your meditation will become deeper and begin to affect the psyche causing opposing feelings and emotions, both positive and negative to surface . This is necessary and will initiate the process of purification.

****

Posture

An equally important factor in creating the right environment for meditation is your sitting position. Keeping the back upright but relaxed is considered the most vital aspect of meditation posture. Remove shoes, belt, and watch.
Sit crossed legged on the floor or on a chair with your back straight.

You do not have to be on the floor but your back should be very straight, the classical meditation positions are excellent because they enable you to sit for longer periods without being distracted by the physical body. If you sit on a chair, refrain from leaning against it to allow a free flow of energies.

The initial stages of meditation are not intended to project you into spectacular states of transcendence, but as previously mentioned in step one, to build up systematically and later, to achieve true, inner peace. If you can sit comfortably in the lotus position this is ideal. Once your knees, hips and ankles gain sufficient flexibility you will find the lotus relaxing. Never force your limbs into the lotus as you can easily damage your knees. Maybe you can begin in the half lotus instead.

" Of all the postures, two are special . The first is the perfect posture, the second is the lotus posture " .
Yoga Sutra, Patanjali

****

Breathing

" When the breath wanders the mind also is unsteady. But when the breath is calmed the mind too will be still, and the yogi achieves long life. Therefore, one should learn to control the breath." ~ Svatmarama, Hath Yoga Pradipika

....
When we breathe, we take in two kinds of energy. The energy drawn in through the left nostril is negative (not in a bad sense but as the opposite to positive energy), and when breathing through the right nostril we draw in positive energy. These two streams of energy meet at the channel of energy running the length of the spine, called, susumna and are then absorbed by the entire subtle nervous system, (nadis) of which there are reputedly 72,000 main arteries. If we can learn to direct them up through the centre of the spinal column, then they will directly activate all psychic centres (chakras).

Meditation is a spiritual practise that requires re-training the brain.

****

Using the breath as a means to helping us achieve this is for most, the best route to take. For your first meditation, you may decide to meditate for ten minutes or so . Make it your intention to pay as much attention as you can to your breathing. The breath should come in through the nostrils and back out through the nostrils.

You will find that this method of breathing will be the most beneficial for inducing a relaxed, meditative state.
Take a few deep breaths, then let the breath flow out naturally. Focus on the rhythm of the breath and on the air you breathe.
Allow your thoughts to come and go without paying any attention to any one thought, stay focused on your breath. Do not become agitated by your thoughts, just notice them and return to concentrating on your breathing.
As your mind becomes quiet and still, dwell upon your breath.
Remember, at the beginning, the practise is very much a concentration exercise, it is inevitable that unwanted thoughts will interrupt your practise. This is how you learn to use your willpower.
There are numerous, physical and mental benefits derived from pranayama,(a Sanskrit word prana, meaning breath, and yama its cessation) including increased vitality and alertness; the removal of toxins: better sleep; better digestion through the gentle massaging of internal organs and intestines; more oxygen in the bloodstream; strengthened lungs; the control and elimination of stress; better speech; and improvement of skin tone. Yoga breathing will improve concentration, memory, confidence and, psychic ability.
These benefits have been well documented, but the main purpose of pranayama, is beyond the purely

physical and mental levels. It is to draw the one, universal energy to you at an etheric level in abundance so that it can be used to enhance your spiritual development.

Breath counting can be of great assistance here.

Count mentally to yourself on the out breath, starting with two counts and slowly build up to no more than five.

The act of breath counting will strengthen your resolve to stay focused within.

Stay totally present in the moment, not thinking of past or future events.

Be one with your breath. Look deeply into your breath. The very act of breathing out is a letting go. It's a release, an expulsion of any negativity we may be carrying inside.

When we learn the value of the exhalation breath our daily lives are transformed.

Your breath is the key to mindful meditation. We rarely give our breath a second thought and yet it is our most fundamental and powerful healing tool.

As we begin to experience profound changes in the way we think and feel, we then learn to fully appreciate just how crucial the very act of "breath awareness" is to our overall well-being.

It is impossible to feel anger when the breath is under your control, flowing with a gentle, even rhythm.

We breathe approximately 23,000 times in a single day and depending on your size, sex and physical and mental state, the average volume of air taken in with each breath is about 20 cubic inches.

But with proper attention given to your breathing this volume may be increased to 100 to 130 cubic inches per breath, therefore providing you with five times the oxygen, and ridden you of five times the carbon dioxide.! Many alternative practitioners are now using oxygen therapy to treat illness and disease with amazing results.

So by learning techniques that will supply your brain and body with the ethereal substance of oxygen you will begin to notice a significant, beneficial change to your overall health and mental disposition.

"And when the body is in silent steadiness, breathe rhythmically through the nostrils with a peaceful ebbing and flowing of breath. The chariot of the mind is drawn by wild horses, and those wild horses have to be tamed."   Svetasvatara Upanishad

Chapter Four

Concentration-Mantras- Pineal Gland

Concentration is the result of directed thought. Whenever thought is directed to or on a specific place or thing – that frame of mind is then termed as concentration.
The action of concentration is a prerequisite to meditation, you must acquire the ability to concentrate. Concentration is the act of holding attention steady. We all concentrate in numerous ways throughout the day but perhaps, do not recognize it as such. For example reading a book, playing tennis, watching a film all require a level of concentration. Driving a car, after a while, becomes automatic and requires very little attention.
The practise of concentration on an object is never automatic, it must be continually deepened through gentle effort.
The great teachers of yoga and meditation tell us that these practises all lead toward an inner centre – the core of our being – and that by fixing our attention it is possible to know that centre directly. Concentration they say, will lead us there. But in order to practise concentration we need an object on which to rest our attention. We also need to understand the basic methods of practise.
During meditation a veritable train of thoughts, feelings, impressions, sensations, desires and

memories pass through the mind. We can either allow ourselves to become distracted by them or remain simply watching.

When our awareness becomes firmly centred on the object of meditation, a strong resting place is created. We observe our mental activities from an increasingly stable centre of self-observation and do not become engaged with the thoughts that pass by.

The object we choose to focus on for concentration may be external – a candle flame, flower, photograph of a loved one. Or it can be something or a concept that inspires us.

For twelve seconds try keeping your mind on a single point, a few inches in front of your third eye, (the space between the eyebrows), for example.

Visualize that potential "third eye"; consider the benefits of connecting to that mystical part of you. Meditate on every aspect of it. To do so for twelve seconds is called Dharana, if continued with unhampered focus for twelve times twelve seconds, that is then called Dhyana, or true meditation.

Yogic philosophy teaches that once you learn this, the next stage is Samadhi, a state of super-consciousness, infinite bliss.

Most begin by focusing on the breath.

Concentration on the breath leads from body to mind, and within.

As you continue to watch the breath, become aware of the feeling of cleansing that occurs with each exhalation and the feeling of nourishing that takes place with each inhalation.
By becoming absorbed in your breath this way you will deepen and stabilize your intent to make meditation a daily part of your life bringing tranquillity and greater clarity in place of stress and confusion.
By lengthening the breath we can lengthen our lives, shallow breathers shorten their lives.

" The void is not silent. I have always thought of it more as a transitional space, an in-between space….I have always been interested as an artist in how one can somehow look again for that very first moment of creativity where everything is possible and nothing has actually happened " .Anish Kapoor in conversation with H.K. Bhabha

Mantras are specialized sounds that we give voice to, either alone or as a group to assist us in reaching a higher state of consciousness. There are hundreds of mantras originating from both Yogic and Buddhist sources. They are essentially words possessing spiritual power.
Of all the mantras, the sacred sound of AUM is recognized as the least complicated. In its simplicity it holds a clear, clean resonance that reverberates up and down the length of the spine and with practise can rest and focus on the point of the pineal gland between the eyebrows, the ajna chakra (more about chakras in step six). The importance of the pineal gland in meditation cannot be emphasized enough. The pineal gland is part of the endocrine system and is situated between the two hemispheres of the brain, just above and behind the pituitary gland. With growing awareness of this mysterious gland we are able to connect to our higher self, that part of us that has all the answers we seek if we'd only stay still for long enough to listen.
As the sound of AUM permeates the pineal gland it nudges it awake, for most of earths population it is in a state of inertia.
I believe that this awakening of the pineal gland will play a crucial role in the 21st Century, it is no coincidence that the ajna chakra embodies unconditional truth.
Truth on our planet right now is in very short supply and with our sincere intention to connect to this divine

gland we can help reverse the torrent of world-wide, governmental lies, secrecy and deceit. Truth is synonymous with love, both of which can heal and are contagious.

To arouse the pineal gland takes time and patience, its progress can be slow, but eventually all obstructions to further enlightenment will fall away.

The sound of Aum acts as a sacred tool helping to chip away at perceived blocks to a higher consciousness akin to the resonance of ultrasound as it destroys unwanted or negative thoughts .

To produce the sound of AUM you need to be seated comfortably with closed eyes and regular, nostril breathing until you feel relaxed.

Begin by humming strong enough to create a vibration that reaches the top of your head.

You may need to repeat this several times at first. Your hum should feel steady and even as it rises up into the skull.

After a short time begin to extend the sound down to the solar plexus (Manipura chakra) feeling its resonance more intensely, after taking an in-breath and with mouth open begin to sound the AUM as you release the breath from below the navel drawing the sound upward into the throat, when it reaches the roof of the mouth it then vibrates into the head. The AUM ends softly as the lips close.

Repeat several times. Allow it's vibration to amplify the electromagnetic field around you as it gently fades away.
Although it is very difficult to convey sound through the written word, the AU of AUM is pronounced as in audit.
The M part becomes an elongated hum as the lips come together gently as you expel the last fragment of breath.
Revel in the sound of your voice for it is as individual as your fingerprint.
The mantras were devised by the advanced spiritual masters of the past who observed the sounds made by their psychic centres (chakras), as prana flowed through them. They knew through experimentation, that the repetition of these mantras would enhance the natural flow of prana through the chakras of any individual who recited them, thus enabling the chakras to open, improving concentration, bringing inspiration and harmonizing the different subtle bodies of the practitioner, drawing them closer towards meditation and self-realization.
By meditating on the AUM, one is lifted up into higher states of consciousness and united with the supreme spiritual reality. Placing your concentration on the sound current will direct your individual consciousness back to its source in omnipresent cosmic consciousness.
Meditation on the sound current is considered one of the highest forms of meditation. This form of

meditation is directly related to the highest chakra, the sahasraram or thousand petal lotus at the crown of the head.

"Mantra becomes one's staff of life and carries one through every ordeal. Each repetition has a new meaning, carrying you nearer and nearer to God."
Mahatma Gandhi 1869 - 1948

Chapter Five

Chakra Awareness

What are chakras? Perceived wisdom from down the ages tells us that wherever dynamic energies converge in nature they form whirling, circular patterns or vortices. The chakras can be thought as being the interface between the inner light and the Universal Mind.
The ancient vedic seers understood that similar vortices occurred within the human body and described them as: when two or more channels of subtle energy meet that melding is called a vortex, and named them 'chakra, meaning 'wheel'.
This concentrated energy is known to posses spiritual qualities and appeared to the seers to be multi-coloured. They saw seven main chakras that seemed to reflect the health and the spiritual condition of people. Now, in recent times the chakras are said to be the colours of the rainbow, with each chakra consisting of one of these colours. Kirlian photography has confirmed the existence of the auric field, which can contain all the colours of the rainbow, as do the chakras.

Muladhara – The base chakra – red
Svadistana - The sacral chakra - orange
Manipura - The solar plexus chakra – yellow
Anahata - The heart chakra - green
Vishuddha - The throat chakra - blue
Ajna   - The brow chakra - indigo
Sahasrara - The crown chakra - violet

Most people with an interest in meditation will already have some knowledge of the chakras. We all know that we are much more than a physical body and that we have subtle bodies of energies that create an energy field that surrounds us. Kirlian photography confirms the existence of these energy fields (bio-photons).
To really learn all there is to know about chakras would take years of study and many books have been written for this purpose alone, however, when one believes them to exist and they become part of your reality it then becomes possible to meditate upon a particular chakra to manifest specific desires pertaining to your chosen chakra.

For example, the base chakra, <u>muladhara</u>, is synonymous with 'grounding'. The more grounded we become the less our problems appear. This chakra is about self-preservation and instinctual behaviour. By drawing our attention to our base chakra we can release our fears and negativity and overcome difficulties that once seemed insurmountable: it gives us a new perspective of life .

The sacral chakra, <u>svadistana</u>, is associated with consciousness of our sexuality, emotions and sensuality. It is related to the sacral vertebrae in the spine, the sacral plexus of nerves and the sex glands – the ovaries and testicles.

<u>Manipura</u>, the solar plexus chakra, means "city of gems". It is referred to as the centre of identity and selfhood.

The solar plexus is connected to the digestive system and to the assimilation of food and nutrients and also to the assimilation of knowledge and experience .

The heart chakra. <u>Anahata</u> is allied to compassion, love of others and a love of God, or if preferred, Creator or All That Is.

****

By bringing our attention to the heart we develop a healthy love of our self which enables us to reveal our vunerability and tenderness towards others.

Heart centred meditation is an extremely necessary habit to acquire to counter balance the lack of love felt by so many of Earth's inhabitants.

<u>Vishudda</u>, the throat chakra means "pure" and is foremost affiliated with communication, to find one's voice and be heard, literally and metaphorically. Working with the throat chakra will help you become more attuned to what your body is telling you, more aware of the body's needs to create a healthy, internal environment that will nurture your spiritual growth.

<u>Ajna</u>, the brow chakra, ajna means "command". Through awakening this chakra we can achieve command of our lives. The brow centre awakens a need to enjoy the completeness of inner harmony of body, mind, emotions, spirit and soul.

The crown chakra, <u>sahasrara</u> is connected to the pituitary gland which regulates the endocrine system. It is concerned with openness. When our attention is focused on our crown chakra it allows us to move beyond the physical universe to the universal sources of energy and information. Here it is possible to link to the cosmic intelligence that holds all of the answers we are seeking.

We each have a psychic body known as the aura. This is an energy body composed of spiritual or etheric matter. It extends several inches from the physical body where the psychic centres or chakras are

contained, interconnecting with a network of channels known as the nadis. Sanskrit text's refers to 72,000 nadis that produce a constant flow of etheric energy, in and around the aura interconnecting major and minor psychic centres.
It is said that when integration of all the chakras takes place then illumination is reached.

"When, in meditation, the true nature of the
object shines forth, not distorted by the mind
of the perceiver, that is absorption (Samadhi) Patanjali
Yoga Sutras

****

Here I will expand further on how meditation can help protect us from EMF's and other negative forces. With dedication and an ability to sustain a regular practise you will have the tools to listen better to the still, quiet voice within. You will awaken the part of you that underlies your thoughts and feelings. You will know how to be more present in the moment. You'll be conscious of the love and wisdom felt at the heart centre and with the recognition of your true essence you can live a more fulfilling and caring life.

Human consciousness is evolving more rapidly than ever before and we are discovering more about the self by the day, perceiving ourselves to be much more than just physical bodies, with good reason, as we are connected to the universe through non-physical dimensions and an invisible sea of information.

It has been long established that we are electromagnetic beings but what is less known is that our electrical systems change when we experience different energy fields thus making the man-made EMF's that we are being saturated with a huge cause for concern. They are literally, altering the structure of our DNA and we have no idea as to how this unwelcome action will affect future generations.

But as we repeatedly turn our thoughts and attention inwards and begin to communicate with the wondrous events taking place within our very cells, it causes a strengthening of the cells membrane making them far more able to cope with any outside interference from synthetic EMF's.

This information can be backed up by the research done by David Sereda and a book he has written entitled "The Electro-Magnetic Human".
He talks of how the cells membrane is adversely affected by abnormal amounts of radiation (phone masts, mobile phones, wi-fi technology, etc;) which breaks the membrane wall causing death to the cell.
I firmly believe that the daily practise of meditation can protect us from this onslaught of manufactured EMF's, as the efficacy of meditation acts as the consummate filter.
It is also my belief that this smog of electromagnetic contamination is altering our very DNA. Although DNA is said to be immortal, it can still become damaged, meditation will help restore it.

****

Many things have been written about 2012, which is just months away and according to some, there is another real threat facing us, and that is that there will be events, orchestrated by the few that thrive on creating chaos and fear, that will lead to the collapse of the entire electromagnetic grid of the country (world?).

Our lives will literally be turned upside down, we will be ripe for manipulation by those in power that would benefit from our confusion.

The 2012 Olympics is thought to be at the centre of this plan. We will see. But knowing that we are electromagnetic ourselves it does deserve some thought and makes the argument for meditation, the defender of our psyche, even more compelling.

Down through the ages, mystics the world over have kept their knowledge for initiates of various secret societies. This was to prevent people who were not ready to receive this information which could be misunderstood or misused.

However, there were those who withheld their knowledge to keep the power to themselves rather than sharing it with others with the intention of using it for their own selfish purposes: 'The Illuminati', 'Secret Societies', 'Freemasons', right up to the present shadowy figures behind global, governmental decision making.

This became known as the "left-hand path" or "black magic".

Secrecy surrounding this ancient wisdom, first arose in the earliest known texts on Earth-the Sanskrit Vedas and was handed down orally.

It concerned the true spiritual nature of mankind, the origin of the universe and the evolutionary journey of all life and was regarded as a key to awakening the spiritual potential of anyone who heard and understood it.

This early knowledge is available to us today through dedication to the practise of meditation. With regular practise of sitting in stillness coupled with the immense increase in solar activity that is causing our computer-brain to upgrade and our DNA to alter, we are able to tap into the infinite reservoir of intelligence that lies within.

These higher levels of solar energy are expected to peak in 2012. There is scientific evidence that the increase in the solar activity could give a significant boost to human consciousness and to spiritual evolution, opening the door to a new era.

This is because we, human beings, constantly generate electromagnetic fields around us depending on the thoughts and feelings we have. The sun interacts directly with our DNA and stimulates changes in biosynthesis in cells. Only those who have developed sufficiently will be able to withstand the cosmic bombardment.

I therefore think that when we have done the inner work necessary, and strengthened our EM field in the process, combined with the suns energetic assistance, we will be prepared for a magnificent, long-awaited spiritual advancement .

It is God's law that time spent doing spiritual practises is never wasted.

As more and more people are becoming wise about alternative healing that view disease from the perspective of the human spirit, or the body's life-force, the orthodox approach to the human body, that isolates disease to specific body parts seems quite outdated and in urgent need of review.

The use of vibrational medicine in alternative therapy is based upon the idea that we are all unique energy systems and is a blend of both present and ancient beliefs about health and illness, and the body's inner capacity to heal.

The bio-chemical molecules that make up the physical body are a form of vibrating energy. During meditation our energetic vibration speeds up, increasing our energy level, we become higher vibrational beings. We change our energetic field.

The destructive, electromagnetic spectrum of the 3rd Millenium, surrounds us and permeates our cells, weakening the immune system and exposing us to ill health.When we function on a higher vibrational plane at cellular level whilst meditating, we counterbalance the negative consequences of these harmful rays. Combining this knowledge with vigilance to what you think, eat and drink will cause a valuable transformation in your perspective of life as well as manifesting a powerful shield of protective energy capable of deflecting any noxious rays.

When meditating, acknowledge that everything that you wish to achieve is all "for the highest good." To evolve spiritually means coming from a place of love and serving others less fortunate than yourself.

****

"People travel to wonder at the heights of mountains, at the huge waves of the sea, at the long courses of rivers, at the vast compass of the ocean, at the circular motion of the stars; and they pass by themselves without wondering".   St Augustine

Chapter Six

Yoga and Weight-loss

Gain Insight – Lose Weight

This section, was written for those of you in any doubt as to the effectiveness of yoga to induce weight loss. It will also be of considerable help to regular practitioners of yoga who, no-matter how much they exercise still have difficulty in shifting unwanted weight.
Having endured endless taunts through-out my younger life from siblings and friends pertaining to my weight, I truly am empathetic to anyone who has known, or, is in a similar situation.
I was forever being told that I was fat and that I had "big bones", implying that there wasn't a thing I could do about it, that 'Granny Healey' was like it and "that it was all in the genes."
Well, thankfully, I discovered what a lot of nonsense that is.
We think that only a punishing exercise regime will help shed those extra pounds, and that Yoga just couldn't compete. Well it seems as if this notion too is completely without foundation and that through the regular practise of Yoga you really can lose weight.
It was around the age of twenty that I began to lose weight without too much thought, I was happy

working as a croupier at the London Playboy Club and really enjoying life.
But by the time I'd reached my late-twenties, the fast paced life I was leading caught up with me and I became seriously ill with, not one, but two grave illnesses.
It was only then that I learned about the importance of healthy eating and drinking. I must stress that we should seek to lose weight for health and spiritual reasons rather than for vanity.
I cured myself of both pleurisy and hepatitis without any medical intervention, but through diet, yoga and meditation.
Then began an amazing journey which led me to some of the most beautiful places on earth and also to meet a lot of incredible people. I learned all I could about nutrition and began to practise yoga daily. My interest in spiritual matters grew exponentially. I looked and felt ten years younger, there was no going back.
In this part I will teach you how to control overeating through a series of tried and tested breathing exercises that will not only propel you toward abundant health but will also instil in you the means to systematically under-eat: the only way possible to an ever-lasting slimmer you.

But first a little background to this extraordinary, health enhancing practise, of which I've participated for over thirty years.

The word 'Yoga' literally means 'yoke', to unite the individual spirit with the Universal Spirit, or God. One definition of yoga is that it is a method by which to obtain control over one's latent powers, it offers the means to reach self-realization.

Yoga has developed and been perfected over the centuries by the Sages and Wise Men of ancient India who knew well the importance of inhabiting a healthy body. Through the consistent practise of the yoga postures (asanas) they remained lithe and youthful long into old age.

Prolonged practise of yoga will inevitably lead to spiritual awakening, but I will dwell mostly on the physical attributes that can be attained.

You will see incredible improvements in your health, your appearance and your vitality.

Yoga is not a religion or a philosophy. It is a scientific, spiritual training, the goal being to enable us to realize the divinity of our own true nature.

There are many different schools of yoga, here are just some of them:

Ashtanga Yoga, is a fast paced, gymnastic type of yoga which suits practitioners in the West as they make the transition from the gym to the yoga mat. Founded in 1948 by Pattabhi Jois.

Bikram Yoga was created by Bikram Choudry after being told he would never walk again at the age of twenty following a weight lifting accident. He created his own series of postures to regain his own health and now teaches it to others. The poses are very demanding and are performed in a heated room to allow muscles, ligaments and joints to stretch more easily.

B.K.S Iyengar is the founder of Iyengar Yoga, he is now in his nineties and still practising daily. His book "Light on Yoga" in 1966 had a great influence worldwide and now over 500,000 people in the UK alone practise this method .

Kundalini Yoga, also called the yoga of awareness and promises to ' help you be the best you can be'. Yogi Bhajan established '3HO', the Healthy Happy Holy Foundation, in 1969, the '3HO' is now a training organization with centres all over the world.

The best known school of yoga in our hemisphere, is Hath Yoga. The name, derived from the Sanskrit Ha, which represents the female principle and Tha, the male principle.
Hatha Yoga consists of hundreds of asanas, all designed to strengthen and purify the body.

It is from the Hatha disciplines that I draw my experience and knowledge from having been trained in the late 1970's by two of the world's most adept teacher's, to both of whom I will be eternally thankful, Ana Forest and Ganga White.
There are other schools of Yoga you may want to explore, Siddha Yoga, Sivananda Yoga, Viniyoga and although Vanda Scaravelli adamantly refused to give her name to a school of yoga, I mention her here because she was an outstanding teacher who inspired hundreds of thousands of people right up to her death in 1999.

Raja Yoga is the yoga of meditation, meditation is the process by which we experience pure consciousness. "By means of meditation higher octaves of spiritual energy are made to flow through the subtle bodies and the mind. Mental and emotional activity cease so that the astral and mental bodies are capable of reflecting, without distraction, then love, wisdom and power will come from the plane of pure consciousness".

∎∎∎

"In health there is freedom. Health is the first of all liberties".
Henri-Frederic Amiel ….1828 - 1881
The ancient Yogis devised a myriad of asanas (physical

postures) to bring us into a state of union with ourselves at a deeper level, thus enabling us to gain control of needless desires, including excessive amounts of food!.

Upon careful observation of the animal kingdom, the original practitioners of Yoga noticed they possessed an amazing ability to, not only relax but to utilize their energies properly and effectively, sleeping at intervals around the clock and eating only according to need they lived to five times their maturity and retained their full vitality for fifth sixth's of their lives. However, for men and women it is a very different story. We live to only twice our maturity and begin to lose our vigor half way through!.

They concluded that the answer to health and longevity was to emulate the way in which the animals used their bodies and to revert back to simple, natural living.

The primary emphasis in all the asanas is on relaxation, it is essential never to strain or force oneself into a position, you learn to relax into each posture slowly.

Hatha Yoga asks for high levels of discipline but there is no need for extremes. There are a lot of good teachers around, find one that you feel comfortable with and practise as often as you can.
With patience, you'll become more flexible in both body and mind. But remember, the true purpose of a regular practise is to fuse the mental, physical and spiritual bodies and to learn to live to your full capacity.

" To keep the body in good health is a duty, otherwise we shall not be able to keep our mind strong and clear......
Gautama the Buddha...563 BC

Chapter Seven

Systematic-Under-eating

If you have been told that you can eat three full meals a day and remain slim, you have been seriously mislead. Of course this will depend on the amount you eat and the inevitable exceptions to the rule: having a very high rate of metabolising, being extremely athletic or genetically predisposed to natural slimness.
Over-eating and anxiety are the most common causes of sickness and disease. Toxemia and enervation are the underlying causes of all disease whether acute or chronic. Toxins in the body originate from wrong choice of food, worn-out body cells, drugs, unloving thoughts, polluted air and water. Enervation comes from over-activity, noise, radiation, extreme climate, over-eating, sexual excesses, vaccination, toxins stress or rapid detoxification.
In most degenerative disorders, the body is enzyme-exhausted and nutritionally deficient. Lack of enzymes leads to incomplete metabolism. The undigested food must be eliminated as toxins. Waste accumulates from infancy because of toxaemia and enervation, eventually, to a level which may interfere with the functioning of the body.
The strength of your constitution will determine how long it will take to become sick.
The most nutritious diet for the human body is organic, uncooked foods, ie; salads made from alfalfa sprouts,

mixed bean sprouts, grated carrot and beetroot, avocado etc;.
Although this may sound quite austere, when alternated with home-made, nourishing soups cooked with plenty of imagination and flair, this healing diet can be made to taste supremely delicious.
Not only will these wholesome meals be delectable, but when eaten for only a few weeks, your body will return to its most beneficial, healthy, optimal size.
The key is to take it step by step. Don't become daunted by the fact that you'll be denying yourself some of your favourite foods. You can trick your mind into thinking your new, life-changing diet is only temporary and that you can resume your usual diet when you choose to.
Hopefully, however, that shall not be necessary, for, when you experience the tremendous transformation that will undoubtedly take place on all levels of your being there really will be no going back: your skin will glow, your hair become lustrous, all mental faculties enhanced, increased stamina and endurance and much, much more.

"For breath is life, and if you breathe well you will live long on earth."
Sanskrit proverb

Once this magical metamorphosis takes place for you, old habits and desires will simply become insignificant,

> "Every so-called DISEASE is a crisis of Toxemia; which means that toxins have accumulated in the blood above the toleration point, and the crises - the so-called disease – is a vicarious elimination. A cold is driven into chronic catarrh, flu may be forced to take on a n infected state; pneumonia may end fatally if secretions are checked by drugs."
> J.H. Tilden, M.D. Toxemia Explained

you will have reached the point of no return. ! Before you embark on your quest for bodily perfection you should have a good knowledge of yoga practise. The yoga asanas and breathing exercises will have prepared you sufficiently enough to enable you to exert your will over your appetite. We know what we should do to lose weight so why do we lack the will power to put knowledge into action? Will is of divine origin and is easy to execute once we have established a connection to our higher consciousness through meditation and yoga.

When you wish to eat something, stop to consider whether your body really needs it.
During dietary transition the hardest task will be to cut down on the size of meals. Most doctors recognize that over-eating is the greatest killer.
Some of the major causes of over-eating are forced feeding in childhood; anxiety, unnatural diet, poor mastication, enlargement of the stomach from past feasts.
Self-image is important. It develops from the pre-natal period onward. A poor self-image creates anxiety, which is discomforting.
Since anxiety is mainly a mind-emotion activity, anything that reduces the energy level in the brain will also reduce anxiety. When eating, awareness of self and its contrast with the ideal self is lowered; thus anxiety is relieved.
When you were a baby, your mother relieved your anxieties by giving you food. When adult, you try, subconsciously, to duplicate the experience.
Unless the cause of stress and anxiety are dealt with, prolonged tension can cause mental and physical exhaustion.
It is never too late to change your self-image, regardless of past, negative experiences.
Read the inspirational teachings of the great, spiritual master's that have so much to offer, meditate daily, evaluate your current situation, sharing your aspirations will strengthen your resolve to succeed.

"Whatever you can do, or dream you can do, begin it. Boldness has genius, power and magic in it. Begin it now."   Goethe

> " You will not give even an hours rest to me your stomach. Day after day, every hour you keep on eating. You have no idea how I suffer, O trouble making ego. It is impossible to get on with you." ... Osborne

The Yogis were the first to discover the importance of utilizing the breath - the air you breathe, in order to improve the functions of the mind and body. They called it pranayama, from the Sanskrit word prana, meaning breath, and yama, its cessation. They explored pranayama thoroughly, from every angle, including the mystical.

They realized that air nourishes our bodies just as much as food and water. Without a proper supply of oxygen to the blood we are unable to assimilate food or to think clearly, we need it to feed the skin, nerves, tissues, glands and vital organs.

Correct breathing and specific breathing exercises, not only keep you healthy and youthful but also helps you to be supple and slim.

As we grow older, our diaphragm becomes more sluggish, arteries harden and red blood corpuscles become unevenly distributed which causes fat to be accumulated instead of being metabolised and burned up. Deep breathing, with its cleansing and stimulating actions can help to avoid obesity as it improves metabolism which then transforms deposits of fat into body fuel, or added energy.

When breathing exercises are practised and combined with a mental affirmation, the results can be felt in a short time, according to the depth of your sincerity, intent and desire.

The following exercise was devised by Dr George King after studying and practising pranayama for many years. It is designed to create internal harmony by breathing in and out in a measured way. This rhythmic breath will help purify the nervous system and bring about a great feeling of peace and tranquillity.

Sit on the floor or a straight backed chair if that is uncomfortable with your spine erect.

Breathe in slowly and steadily for a count which is within your capacity.

Next, breathe out for the same count, making the inhalation and exhalation of the same duration.

After a little practise, the in and out breaths will, automatically be of equal length.

When this stage has been reached, you can then add the mental affirmation, which should flow in and out without any strain at all.

Use the following, powerful affirmation:

"I AM NOW PURIFYING MY MIND AND BODY."

Practise this exercise for at least 15 minutes a day and you will be truly rewarded for your efforts.
For more information on this and other exercises from Dr George King, please contact the 'The Atherius Society'.

****
****

"The way to eat a lot is to eat little, that way you live long enough to be able to eat a lot"…….Anonymous

The following wisdom is from a remarkable book by Viktorus Kulvinskas, titled "Survival Into the 21st Century". I believe it's out of print now. It was a great teacher to me and taught me most of what I know about the mind and body, and a significant amount of authors of esoteric books that I have read and others about health and nutrition, appear to of gleaned a tremendous amount of information from this distinct publication.

"Try an imaginary binge. Eat with your mind to your stomach's content all the naughty foods you are trying to avoid.

Think about how the food tastes, feels and smells. Feel your stomach expanding, your consciousness diminishing and youth fading. Recall the details of how you felt after a feast. Visualize the kind of disease a congested body can cause. See the composition: lots of calories, nutrition-less starchy white flour, hydrogenated fat, lung destroying pasteurized milk, cancer causing artificial flavourings, nerve-damaging colour additives. Ask yourself: How was this food grown ? on a tree, a bush, or was it created by man in a laboratory. ?

Keep a diary of your daily eating habits. Time, quantity and choice of should be entered. What were the motivating psychological reasons for overeating: anxiety, avoidance, punishing someone. Were you tired and eating for stimulation? How did you feel before and after the meal,? enter your weight daily. Where did you eat ? Was it straight from the

refrigerator, a package or restaurant ? Did you leave tempting foods around the house.?
Before you begin eating you generally still have some sanity about your dietary needs.
On a plate serve as much food as you think you should eat. Take the plate to the dining room.
 Do not go for seconds, or nibble after the meal. Remember, "One extra mouthful will be too much and a hundred will not be enough."

****

Sharing food with others, eating slowly, chewing food thoroughly, being quiet in peaceful surroundings will reduce overeating.
Start each meal with a prayer, chant or meditation. Ask the Omnipresent Spirit for aid in self-mastery.
Think about the strength and health the food is to give you. Visualise yourself in the beautiful body you can gain through self-mastery. Do not read, listen to the radio or watch television.

Concentrate on the Omnipresent as you chew thoroughly your simple meal.
It is best not to indulge in conversation while eating, but if you have company, limit discussion to friendly, loving exchanges, no disputes. Only pleasant thoughts encourage digestion.
Have few preferably unseasoned, selections at a meal. Each new food creates its own hunger by chemical stimulation. Meat satisfies one kind of hunger. If it is followed by bread and butter, new cravings are created and must be satisfied. There is no limit.
Many people eating an inadequate diet, continue to experience hidden hunger even when their stomachs are full. This craving is a sign that the diet lacks certain food vibrations. Unless they are supplied, the individual will develop visible symptoms of deficiency. If hidden hunger remains unsatisfied, the eventual result of ignoring this survival mechanism is chronic disease and death.
To overcome this craving, include in your diet some wheatgrass or raw, fresh vegetable juice, a mixture of sprouted alfalfa and mung beans, sea vegetables and sun.
You can grow wheatgrass easily, by chewing grass between meals, hidden hunger will quickly disappear. Under-eating can increase our physical endurance, clear our heads and give us long life.
In times of crisis when famine is a reality, more people could be fed on less, giving everyone a fair share of the planet's harvest.

The late Dr. Clive McCay of Cornell University doubled the life span of rats by halving their food intake in his experiment in 1927, extending their lives equal to 140 years in human terms. In orthodox geriatric studies, it has been found that a slim body, due to little eating and excellent elimination, is and essential factor for reaching the century mark.
Talking of which, regular elimination of food-wastes from the bowels is crucial to maintaining a healthy mind and body.
This is how Dr William Hunter, London, put it:
"The fact that chronic constipation might exist in certain individuals as an almost permanent condition without apparently causing ill health is due solely to the power and protective action of the liver.
It is only an evidence that some individuals possess the caecum and colon of an ox, with the liver of a pig capable of doing any amount of detoxification."
Accumulated, putrefied hardened waste in the colon, in some cases, for years, places a great strain on the eliminative organs, especially hindering the functioning of the liver and kidney.
A chain reaction develops: fats, proteins and carbohydrates are not properly metabolized; electrolyte balance is upset; the entire body is placed under stress.

"The colon is a sewage system, but by neglect and abuse it becomes a cesspool.
When it is clean and normal, we are well and happy; let it stagnate, and it will distil the poisons of decay, fermentation and putrefaction into the blood. It will poison the brain and nervous system so that we become mentally depressed and irritable; it will poison the heart so that we are weak and listless, poison the lungs so that the breath is foul, poison the digestive organs so that we are distressed and bloated and poison the blood so that the skin is sallow and unhealthy.
In short, every organ of the body is poisoned, and we age prematurely. Look and feel old, our joints are stiff and painful; neuritis, dull eyes and a sluggish brain overtake us; the pleasure of living is gone." V.E. IRONS, INC.
Not a very savoury description, but true none-the-less. A clean and healthy colon plays an essential role in creating a new you.
You'll need a strong desire and willingness to recover your health through natural means, but it is the only way to regain, full health.
Use enemas, have colonic irrigation, fast on fresh juices for a few days, get out to the park, sea or river, away from the city whenever possible, drastically reduce the amount of time spent in front of the TV; TV slows down your evolutionary progress and is a form of frequency control, these things done in conjunction with yoga and meditation will have

monumental affect on your entire psyche, elevating you to another level of being.
p.s. as much as I adhere to a lot of this advice, I feel that it's incredibly important to treat yourself to your favourite, naughty foods occasionally as I do.

"Without health, life is not life; it is only a state of languor and suffering."
- Francois Rabelais

Chapter Eight

Your Second Brain

We have all experienced the fluttering sensation in our gut in anticipation of something about to happen and more than likely and you may have realized that it was allied to your thoughts, well, an exciting book called "The Second Brain " by Dr Michael Gershon, Chairman of Anatomy and Cell Biology at Columbia University College of Physicians and Surgeons, gives us the first concrete evidence of the biological connection between our brain and our gut (esophagus, stomach, small intestine and colon).
Dr Gershon refers to the entire gastrointestinal system as " the body's second nervous system," called the enteric nervous system.
This primitive nervous system, located in our intestinal tract, is incredibly complex. It consists of hundreds of millions of nerve cells – more than all the rest of the body put together – and is colonised by thousands of different species of micro flora.
When our second brain is suffering, mental disorders, obesity, hormonal disturbances, addiction, depression, can all develop . For it is responsible for maintaining the biological terrain that protects us from illness and degeneration.
During early fetal development both your gut and brain grow from the same mass of embryonic tissue.

When that piece of tissue divided, one part grew into your central nervous system (your brain and cranial nerves)). The other section became your enteric nervous system (your "gut" brain.)
During later stages of fetal development, these two brains then became connected via the vegus nerve. The vagus nerve is the longest of all our cranial nerves, and creates a direct connection between your brain and gut.
Because of this link, the condition of your gut has a profound influence on your psychological well being. Nearly every brain-regulating chemical found in your brain has also been found in your gut brain – including both hormones and neurotransmitters.
Approximately 90 percent of the body's serotonin (a feel-good chemical or neurotransmitter) is located in the cells of the gut, where it is used to regulate intestinal movements. The remainder is to be found in the central nervous system where it has various functions.
These include the regulation of mood, appetite, sleep and muscle contraction.
Serotonin also has some cognitive functions, including in memory and learning.
"The brain is not the only place in the body that's full of neurotransmitters," Dr. Gershon explains.

" one hundred million neurotransmitters line the length of the gut – approximately the same number found in the brain."
As research on the circuitry between our two brains progresses, neuro-scientists are understanding more and more about how we act and feel.
The name given to this area of science is ' neurogastroenterology, ' and since the publication of "The Second Brain " in 1998, it has attracted a lot of interest from Dr Gershon's peers and layman alike.
The inclusion of this information in this book is because it is a fundamental component of the understanding of the physical body. If we are to address and conquer our needless wants and desires, which is prerequisite for our spiritual awakening, we must first discover what is causing them.
We now have an idea of the crucial role that the gut plays in our general health, it's therefore necessary for me to point out the dangers of alcohol consumption. From a physical point of view it is thought that the occasional drink is not harmful. However, on the spiritual side it can severely hamper your progress. Here's what the 'Theosophical Society' has to say about alcoholic beverages: "They are worse for his moral and spiritual growth than meat, for alcohol in all its forms has a direct, marked and very deleterious influence on man's psychic condition.
Wine and spirit drinking is only less destructive to the development of the inner powers, than the habitual use of Hashish, opium, and similar drugs."

From the purely, physical standpoint, if we are serious in our intentions to change our negative patterns of behaviour then alcohol consumption is best cut to the bare minimum, or, ideally it should be avoided altogether.

Yeast feeds on sugars and carbohydrates which turn into sugar. They produce chemical wastes during fermentation that contain high levels of ethanol – alcohol. This is why some people that abstain from the use of alcohol appear to live in a state of drunkenness that altars consciousness. As the alcohol produced by the yeast breaks down it creates a poisonous chemical named acetaldehyde. Acetaldehyde is six times more toxic to the brain than ethanol itself, which insidiously undermines brain functions and damages neurological structures.

Here is yet another example of how the gut and brain interact and affect one another.

High levels of acetaldehyde promotes addiction to toxic substances like cigarettes and drugs because of its ability to combine in the brain with dopamine and serotonin.

Many experts believe that acetaldehyde is responsible for other addictions not apparently chemical in origin, such as eating disorders and compulsive behaviour.

Doesn't knowing this make you want to immediately stop all self-destructive actions and work towards renewing every one of the approximately, ten trillion, glorious cells that constitute your magnificent body. ?

"There are two great medicines: Diet and Self-Control."
Max Bircher, 1962

Chapter Nine

Trust Your Body

About six years ago I decided to detox my body by way of a six day liver cleanse. I had fasted in the past so restricting my food intake was not too difficult. Just prior to detoxing I had received a thorough medical check-up at a prestigious health clinic in Knightsbridge, London.
My blood, skin, vision, stress level, heart rate, cholesterol, and hair had all been painstakingly analyzed with the latest technological apparatus. And although I lead as healthier a life as possible, the results were still, quite astounding, I was scientifically proven to be fifteen years younger biologically as opposed to my chronological age, which was then fifty four, I felt elated, all of the work that I had done on myself in the previous years had paid off.
The purpose of this latest cleanse was to release the stones from my kidneys, gall-bladder and liver without medical intervention. Because despite being in sound health, I knew from researching this subject and the fact that I had not always been so attentive to my body's needs, that the above organs were undoubtedly embedded with all manner of toxic waste that over time form into hard stones. Approximately twenty percent of the world's population will develop gall stones at some stage in their lives. The vast majority will choose to have them surgically removed.

But owing to my extreme faith in my body's ability to heal itself, and ignoring concerned friends and members of my family's advice, I was convinced that I should proceed with a liver cleanse.
I was not disappointed. It proved to be another life-changing event.
I had learned yet again from first hand experience just how much of a marvel this fantastic, organic- computer we call the human body is.
I heartily recommend that you to try it for yourselves.
I followed the instructions from a book by Andreas Moritz called 'The Amazing Liver and Gallbladder Flush.' Although I'd first read about it back in 1975 when I was introduced to the work of the aforementioned Viktorus Kulvinskas. I'm legally bound to tell you that you should check with your doctor before embarking on anything of this nature.
Please see the following picture of what I released from my supposedly, healthy body and imagine what an unhealthy person is carrying within them. !
Gallstones come in different sizes, colour and shape. The lightest colour being the newest and dark green stones the oldest. Some are calcified and others contain heavy, toxic substances, all are extremely detrimental to your well-being.
By adhering to the directions correctly of the book mentioned above, the stones will become soft making it possible for them to be discharged without pain.

On the sixth night of the cleanse you have to drink a concoction made up of grapefruit and olive oil immediately upon going to bed. Believe me, by this stage I was so hungry that it tasted like nectar ! Dr; Moritz explains in his book, that upon laying down and placing your hands on your abdomen you will feel the stones rippling away from the affected organs and making their way to the front of the body ready for elimination the following morning.
Well knowing all I know about my own body I was just a tad sceptical but did as he suggested anyway.
I lay in disbelief with my hands strategically placed as I felt what seemed like lots of ball-bearings or marbles rolling towards my groin. It was a very humbling experience, as I realized that we never, ever stop learning about the incredible abilities of the human body to heal itself.

This is what was discharged from my body after completing the liver cleanse in 2006. It's like performing surgery on yourself without the pain and the scars. ! I decide to have another go a few months later which produced even more stones, and remember this is from a body that has been confirmed to be fifteen years young biologically and in full health.

I just had to give it another go not long after because you are told that there will undoubtedly be a few remaining stones left behind from your first liver cleanse, right again .!

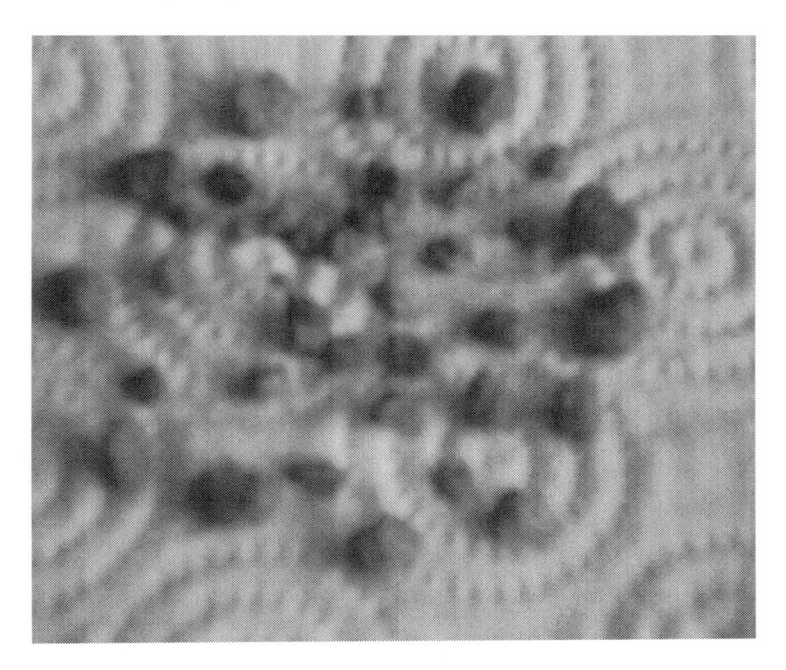

After a second cleanse a few months following the first one

"The greatest of follies is to sacrifice health for any other kind of happiness."

Arthur Schopenhauer

Chapter Ten

Science and Consciousness

We have become so far removed from our 'original source', ventured so far from who we really are that the only direction left for us now is to turn within, to that inner spark of light that is so closely allied to our Creator/Universal Mind/God.
Those who have been meditating steadily for awhile will, most likely have a strong sense of this majestic, magnetic connection.
Cutting edge science acknowledges the existence of consciousness, but have yet been unable to define it. This is because consciousness is not to be found in the 'brain'. It is etheric, not physical.
Scientists themselves term this mystery as 'the hard problem'.
Some scientific theories hold that it comes from, or is even identical to, electrical and chemical processes known to unfold in the brain. Others say it arise elsewhere: in some even subtler, yet undiscovered brain processes, or perhaps a mind-stuff quite distinct from the brain – some call it a soul. None of them have a definitive answer.
Consciousness is awareness beyond mind, everything is consciousness experienced on many different levels depending on how connected we are to 'All That Is'. It is a part of us that is aware of the 'self'.

When you become 'conscious' in life, you attune to the intuitive you, you know instinctively what is right and what is wrong, what to do or what not to do, it all becomes effortlessly apparent, you are no longer reliant on the 'mind' for answers. You trust yourself. You are in sync with the 'Universal Intelligence'.
Every thought we have, directly affects the auric field and consequently our mental and emotional health. We must aspire to elevate the quality of our thoughts, letting go of unnecessary fear and anxiety, aspiring to thoughts of happiness and contentment. A sense of humour is essential for us to reach this state of being, don't take anything in this life too seriously, least of all your self.
This is what David R. Hamilton PhD has to say in his book 'It's The Thought That Counts': "Body and mind are intertwined. Every thought, feeling and intention you have sends ripples throughout your body. The results depend upon the nature of those thoughts, feelings and intentions. They can be so powerful that they even affect your genes. A particular gene that might produce a disease or protect you from disease, for example, can be switched on and off according to how you process the daily experiences of your life. The implications of this are enormous. Every function of the human body is susceptible to thoughts and feelings."

Despite the 21st Century being plagued by wars and chaos, it really is a very exciting and challenging time to be alive. You have chosen to be here at this uncertain, epoch-making period of life on this planet for your spiritual development.
Our bodies contain 120 billion miles of DNA (deoxyribonucleicacid), DNA is the body's genetic library which is present in every cell.
It has been found to be a crystalline structure, therefore is also a receiver and transmitter of energy or light.
Scientist's have yet to discover what over 90% of DNA is for, only approximately 10% of its codes are known. It contains over a hundred trillion times more information than our most advanced technology is capable of.
In David Icke's book, 'Infinite Love is the Only Truth Everything Else is Illusion', he writes "DNA is the foundation of physical form.
What we think of as 'physical' is actually a holographic illusion, and the base form of DNA, as with everything, is a frequency field, a sort of floppy disc or CD holding the genetic program. We need to think in computer terms to understand most simply how it all works".
That's exactly what we are, an organic computer, receiving and transmitting frequencies.
Karl Pribram, a neurophysiologist at Stanford University realised" that the objective world does not exist, or at least not in the way that we are accustomed to believing. What is 'out there' is a vast

ocean of waves and frequencies and reality looks concrete to us only because our brains are able to take this holographic blur and convert it into sticks and stones and other familiar objects that make up our world...."
He states that research from many laboratories by sophisticated analysis of temporal and/or spatial frequencies demonstrates that the brain structures sight, hearing, taste, smell and touch holographically. He continues: "that the brain employs a holographic process to abstract from a holographic domain that transcends time and space."
Every piece of a hologram is an exact representation of the whole and will reconstruct the entire image.
There is no greater example of this than the human body. It is said that
the body is a huge cell encasing the 50 to a 100 trillion cells contained within and that each cell replicates the body, just like a hologram.
The same principle as the phrase "As above, so below.

" A radical inner transformation and rise to a new level of consciousness might be the only real hope we have in the current global crisis brought on by the dominance of the Western mechanistic paradigm"..............

Stanislav Grof

About the Author

Dear Reader, for over thirty years I have devoured countless books covering the subjects of this publication: meta-physics, nutrition, anatomy and healing.
My eyes were first opened whilst living in Los Angeles California in 1975 to 1983. There could not have been a better time to of lived there, I feel blessed for the experience. I encountered so many life-changing moments that have made a lasting impression.
I studied Yoga at The Centre for Yoga in Hollywood for three years and became a teacher after being tutored by two of the best Yoga instructors in the Western hemisphere: Ana Forrest and Ganga White, who both stimulated my desire to learn about yoga and meditation with their astonishing teaching abilities.
I studied spiritual healing at The College of Psychic Studies in London, UK over a two year period. I attended a 'Sacred Geometry Course' with Bob Frissell, in Canada, after his book 'Nothing in This Book is True, But it's Exactly How Things Are', literally fell from the shelf, into my hands whilst at a healing centre in Thailand.!
I also frequented lectures by the pioneers of nutritional therapies, Paavo Airola, who wrote 'How to Get Well' and Viktoras Kulvinskas the author of 'Survival Into the 21st Century'.
I travelled to outstanding, spiritual-gateway locations whilst on yoga retreats, to places such as the Hawaiian

Island of Maui, Mount Shasta, Santa Barbara, Ankor Wat in Cambodia, Glastonbury, UK, the Sahara Desert and more, where I met with like-minded souls. I was unaware at the time that all of these celebrated spots were constructed upon the same ley-lines encircling the earth.

Far away from the electrically contaminated skies, we would sit under what seemed like trillions of stars and would inevitably discuss the meaning of existence and the inherent, unquenchable, human thirst for sacred wisdom, into the night. I learned well and am never happier than when I am sharing this knowledge with others.

My students have told me that during a class they are aware of a pervasive, uplifting energy filling the room. A great accolade that is testament to the profound changes that have occurred at the innermost level of my being.

This transformation could never of taken place without assistance from a divine source. A source that anyone is capable of tapping into if they are willing to do the work.

I am fully aware of the high amount of fear and anxiety that fill thousands of people living through these chaotic times.

But we can choose to change our old, worn out belief systems that keep us locked into these life-threatening emotions at any time, and gradually exchange them for beneficial, life enhancing thoughts that will facilitate the transition toward higher consciousness.
It is, by no means an easy path but once embarked upon, the rewards will be phenomenal.
You will begin to draw to you others that share your new-found enthusiasm for living, giving you strength and support.
Fear, not hate, is the opposite of love.

****

There is advanced technology on earth right now and it is not being used for the good. There is a real battle for our minds and emotions which is being fought for by those who think of themselves as the 'Master race', to them we are lowly cogs in the wheel to be used as brow-beaten, tax paying consumers.
This technology is being used to extract every piece of biological information from our bodies as possibleThis information, is being shared amongst Google, Microsoft, unknown corporations, global databases and many more.
There is a global microchipping agenda in place – with the ultimate goal of all individuals, through subtle mind manipulation (TV etc;) accepting the insertion of microchip implants.

This will eventually lead to electronically attaching each human being to a global computer bringing us under total control.

I feel that too many of us will have shaken ourselves out of the hypnotic state that has been stealthily induced over the years for that scenario to become a reality.

Read 'Blueprint for a Prison Planet,' by Nick Sandberg, published almost ten years ago, it has turned out to be eerily prophetic, and also research Greg Nikolettos, he has made a very informative DVD on this pernicious subject. But, the ultimate aim of the 'illuminati' is to manipulate consciousness, our consciousness.!

Why do I address this issue in a book about yoga and meditation ?

The answer is that you need to be well informed as to the many unseen, unspoken attacks on our mind's and bodies that are designed to sap our spiritual strength or, in the case of the very young, preventing them from ever having any spiritual awareness in the first place. The gross, sexualising of our children by the education system is a horrific example.

Thousands of people across the world are waking up to the fact that things are definitely not right and are looking for answers. We must begin this search by exploring ourselves from within . And so having intensified the huge potential of your body's cells through yoga and meditation, you will be far better equipped to withstand the impact of deleterious, external forces.

****

For the majority of people it is only when life becomes more of a struggle that they begin to ask questions. When our bellies are full and food and money is aplenty, we carry on, never bothering to think about much else other than what's on TV or what new gadget or outfit we can buy.
Our apathy has permitted the political classes to do as they wish, our compliance has brought us to the dire situation that we are in today.
But the challenges we are experiencing have created the exact conditions necessary for massive change, both inside of ourselves and in the world as a whole. And by intergrating your yoga and meditation practise into your everyday life you become more than capable of coping with this transition.
A truly magical transformation, originating from inside of you will arise.

****

The best analogy I have come across that describes the possibility of the existence of other dimensions, is in David Icke's, 'Tales From the Time Loop', he writes: "We don't live in a 'world' so much as a frequency range; the one that our five-senses can access and perceive and the five-sense range of perception is tiny.

Creation is not structured like a chest of draws, one level on top of another. It is made up of frequencies sharing the same space in the same way that all the radio and television frequencies do. Those broadcast frequencies are not just around your body at this moment, they are sharing the same space. This is possible because they are operating on a different frequency range or wavelength to your body and each other. Only when the frequencies are really close do we get 'interference' and become aware of another station. Apart from that all are oblivious to each other's existence because they literally operate in different frequencies, different 'realities' or 'worlds'. When you tune your radio to a station, say Radio 1, that's what you get. You don't hear Radio 2, 3, or 4 because they are not broadcasting on the wavelength to which your radio is tuned. Move the dial from the frequency of Radio 1 to Radio 2 and now, obviously, you hear Radio 2. But Radio 1 did not cease to broadcast when you moved the dial from its wavelength. It goes on broadcasting – existing – while your focus, your consciousness, is tuned to something else."

A succinct summing up of what I believe to be real.

"The mind, once expanded to the dimensions of larger ideas, never returns to its original size."   Oliver Wendell Holmes

"Magic is believing in yourself, if you can do that, anything can happen"
Johann Wolfgang von Goethe

****

The Energy of Love

Love is the energy that created the Universe and all that is within it. Love is the most powerful energy in the Universe.
Giving and receiving love are the most important acts we can perform. But unless you love yourself unconditionally you cannot expect others to do so, for

love must originate from within first, only then is it able to radiate outward.

So many people today have hardened their hearts, it is visible in their faces, and demeanour, for them, sadly, life for them no longer holds love or magic.

It is up to us, the awakened few to manifest all the love available to us and share it with everyone around us and distribute it through prayer to others. There is urgent need for the healing energy of love in the world, without love there is chaos, fear, hate and anger.

The giving and receiving of love opens doors to greater understanding and acceptance.

Love can transform your life into something extraordinary. There are many paths that can take you there, and meditation and yoga are but just two of them. But with the hundreds of thousands of practitioners worldwide that corroborate there effectiveness, and with first hand experience, I can say with confidence that they work.

We are here on earth to support and help each other, to give our time and love to those in need and to display kindness and compassion.

These things and more will be returned to you tenfold, but that should not be the motive that drives you.

This love is yours for the asking. During meditation make a clear intent to have more love in your life; "Ask, and ye shall receive, Ye have not, because ye ask not." Luke 11.9 Bible.

The vibrational energy of love is very magnetic (it is no coincidence that the word magnetic contains the letters that form 'magic'.) The more you love and accept yourself as you are, the more you attract love from others.

You will manifest loving, empowering and abundant situations in your life.

Love heals and brings peace and joy, compassion, abundance, contentment to everything and everyone.

Love is infinite and can never be exhausted, there is a limitless supply of love available to all.

Relish the feeling of love in your heart and soul as you meditate, absorb it into every cell and atom of your being.

Begin right now to introduce some of the practises presented in this book into your daily life, be discerning about how you spend your time, be generous with your love.

The path of personal ascertainment is a tumultuous, ongoing progress.

I wish you a fantastic journey of self-exploration, because you really are a counterpart of the sole 'Supreme Being', (God,Creator, Source), which resides within, and has been patiently awaiting a glorious reunion with you, to share with you the phenomenal discoveries (buried memories) of who and what you truly are.

This hallowed information, I believe, will be disclosed to the human race in this exhilarating, third millennium as you become a conduit for the free-flow of the eternal Great Universal Mind.
Namaste

" Love is the extension of one self for another."
Source unknown

Bibliography

Realise Your Inner Potential ... Dr George King and Richard Lawrence

The Second Brain. ... Dr Michael Gershon

It's the Thought That Counts ... David Hamilton

Infinate Love is The Only Truth ... David Icke

Survival into the 21st Century ... Viktorus Kulvinskas

Left in the Dark ... Graham Gym and Tony Wright

Nothing in this Book is True but it's Exactly How things Are ... Bob Frissel

Cross Currents ... Dr David Becker

What The Doctors Don't Tell You Vol 15 no 5 (August 2004)

To find out if you live near a source of radiation go to, www.sitefinder.radio.gov.uk

Powerwatch is a non-bias organization that will give you more information, call them on 01353778919

"We can easily forgive a child who is afraid of the dark; the real tragedy of life is when men are afraid of the light."
Plato

" There are two ways to live your life – one is as though nothing is a miracle, the other is as though everything is a miracle"…..Albert Einstein

Little-ol' me in a magazine article five years ago (2006) "It is never too late to be what you might have been"......George Elliot

Janie May Still Copyright 2011

Made in the USA
Charleston, SC
28 July 2011